How
JESUS TAUGHT

THE METHODS AND TECHNIQUES
OF THE MASTER

How
JESUS TAUGHT

THE METHODS AND TECHNIQUES
OF THE MASTER

SISTER REGINA M. ALFONSO, S.N.D.

* . * . *

Illustrated by

Sister Marie Fihn, S.N.D.

ALBA · HOUSE NEW · YORK

SOCIETY OF ST. PAUL, 2187 VICTORY BLVD., STATEN ISLAND, NEW YORK 10314

Library of Congress Cataloging in Publication Data

Alfonso, Regina M.
  How Jesus taught.

  1. Jesus Christ — Teaching methods.   I. Title.

BT590.T5A43   1986   232.9'54   86-10812
ISBN 0-8189-0506-9

Designed, printed and bound in the United States of
America by the Fathers and Brothers of the
Society of St. Paul, 2187 Victory Boulevard,
Staten Island, New York 10314, as part of their
communications apostolate.

---

1 2 3 4 5 6 7 8 9 (Current Printing: first digit)

DEDICATION

Dedicated in gratitude
to all who have taught me,
especially my first and best teachers:
my parents,
Joseph M. (deceased) and Aldemira Benedetti Alfonso, Sr.

FOREWORD

"Will you teach a religion methods course that will do more than just prepare prospective teachers for teaching religion? Can you make the content applicable for teaching everything?"

That request, made to me in 1972, was the beginning of this book of reflections.

How Jesus Taught is an educator's look at the teaching methods and techniques of Jesus, the perfect teacher. The work is the result of twelve years of Scripture-combing and meditation on his system of teaching, combined with my thirty-six years of teaching experience in elementary schools and in teacher education programs at the college level.

The teaching methods of Jesus are just as effective today as they were when he used them. His ideas are applicable for teachers of all levels and all areas of the curriculum, since sound principles built on the knowledge of learning and learners should be applied by any teacher.

I have used much of the material in methods courses and in-service workshops for teachers. The favorable response received on the work has encouraged me to share it with other educators.

I am indebted to
    — the source of all scripture quotes:
      The Society for the Propagation of the Faith
      edition of *Good News for Modern Man*
      (American Bible Society, 1971)

    — Sister Marie Fihn, S.N.D., who has captured the spirit
      of the text in her expressive pen and ink drawings

— deceased Sister Mary Christopher Rohner, S.N.D., whose request began this book

— Jesus, the Master Teacher whose love, life and work continue to inspire all who are responding to his call: "Go Teach!"

SISTER REGINA M. ALFONSO, S.N.D.
Notre Dame College of Ohio
Cleveland, Ohio
March 19,1986

CONTENTS

INTRODUCTION

Imagine yourself with the prospect of choosing a small, elite band of twelve students to become the nucleus of the first school of its kind. This school will be uniquely designed to initiate a new way of life built on some very revolutionary principles. . .

. . . So, select the most capable, qualified twelve you can find within the population of about 21,000 square miles. Undoubtedly, your most valuable personal characteristic is the fact that you can read the heart and mind of every person. . .

What teacher wouldn't make the most of such an opportunity to pick super-students for a self-contained classroom or a homeroom class in this exceptional school!

Those were the facts when the Master Teacher chose his homeroom — the Twelve. Considering all this he made some very surprising choices. . .

   . . .one who would become famous for his doubting, another
      for his denials, and a third for his despair
   . . .two of whom would simply appear on the roster, never
      having said or done anything distinctive enough
      to be recorded
   . . .one who would be embarrassed when recognized as a member
      of the Twelve, who would need the help of another to
      write his own memoirs
   . . .two sets of fishermen brothers
   . . .a tax collector of questionable reputation

. . .a political patriot
. . .two fiery-tempered students whose attitudes would
    require some strong reprimands
. . .one who would never totally accept the Teacher's
    philosophy and who would trigger the events
    leading to the death of the Master and to his own

On the surface, not a very promising group! But he had confidence in them; he knew their potential for growth even though it wouldn't be very obvious to others *during* the three years of schooling. But, just think of the effects of that educational system! The giftedness of each of the Twelve continues to unfold as His Mission is accomplished by students of his students nearly two thousand years later. Talk about retention! Talk about learning outcomes! How did he do it?

A close scrutiny of the Gospels
    reveals Jesus utilizing all the teaching strategies
        modern educators have ''invented'',
    and applying the latest discoveries and theories
        of equally modern psychologists.

He is just as successful
    in both large and small group instruction
    as he is in modified departmentalized
    and team teaching arrangements.

The wide variety of techniques
    he uses with his homeroom group
    would thrill any principal.
And here,
    individualized instruction appears at its finest.

Although there doesn't seem to be any indication
    that he ever wrote a daily lesson plan
    or a long-ranged unit,
        he is prepared to the hilt
        for each encounter with his students,

whether he meets them
by the thousands
or one at a time.

He handles audio-visual aids effectively.
He holds a sticky parent-teacher conference.
He takes his homeroom on field trips,
    and corrects them with both humor
    and sternness.

He gives directions
    (and repeats them several times);
        and he adapts his teaching
        to at least seventeen different settings
            — some of them less than idéal!

His procedures
    in "the September" of his career
        are noticeably different from those
    he uses in "the June" of it.

He adjusts and adapts to slower students
    and to gifted ones.
He varies his plan
    as he faces reluctant learners
    and eager ones,
        the frightened
        and the bold ones,
            the naive ones
            and those who shield their phoniness with masks.

In summary, he confronts the same problems and situations that today's teacher faces. And he has the solutions, ready to share with anyone who takes the time to examine and reflect.

PART ONE

LARGE GROUP INSTRUCTION

Large Group Instruction — Crowds

Part One

LARGE GROUP INSTRUCTION

At least twice
    Jesus' class numbered 4000 and 5000 men,
    plus who-knows-how-many women and children;
and a few other times he taught crowds.

His techniques
    in dealing with the crowds
    that followed him
        should give plenty of suggestions
        for teaching a class in September;

for the qualities of "crowd"
    are quite similar to those
    of the "class" we face
        in the beginning of the year,
        before personalities
            have had a chance to jell
            into a cohesive team.

The individuals in his motley crowd
    differed in cultural and political background,
    in attention span,
    and even in purpose
        for being present in that gathering.

Though many must have been there
    because of sincere interest
    and desire to learn;
how many others had come
    to satisfy curiosity
    or to entrap the speaker?
How many came
    because there was nothing else to do,
    or perhaps at the invitation of a friend?

And there probably were at least some
    easily-distracted young people among them
    ". . . because my mother made me come".

Jesus must have been encouraged
    as he looked into eager eyes
        enthralled with his Good News.
And, perhaps he felt a bit annoyed
    as he noticed animated business transactions
        on the outskirts of the crowd.

However, the sight of darting, giggling youngsters
    playing tag among the long robes
    and sandaled feet of his audience
        would have pleased him
        — since he never tried to TEACH them.

He simply blessed them,
    and left their instruction
        to their parents!

Jesus faced people
    of all ages and mental abilities,

all degrees of education
and lack of it.

And what did he do?

. * . * . * .   . * . * . * .   . * . * . * .

Mostly, he told parables
    of wineskins,
        of blind men,
            of wedding feasts,
                of seeds
                    and coins
                        and patches.

With few exceptions,
    Jesus seemed to save the longer
        and more complex parables
            for his smaller groups.

Most of his "crowd" parables
    were only one, two,
    or three verses' worth of thought.

Maybe, because of the poor amplifying system,
    the thoughts had to be rippled
    through the thousands
        after an undulating repetition
        of: "What did he say? I couldn't quite hear him!"

But the content of the couple of sentences is worth looking at.
Examine some of these in detail:

House builders	Lk 6:47-49
Hidden treasure	Mt 13:44
Lamp on a lampstand	Lk 8:16-18

Lost sheep	Lk 4:7
Mustard seed	Mt 13:31-32
Patches on cloth	Mt 9:16
Pearl	Mt 13:45-46
Wedding feast	Mt 9:15
Yeast	Lk 13:20-21
Worthless salt	Mk 9:50

Each one is short,
    to the point;
        and it connects
        a common everyday item or experience
            to an eternal truth.

And the result?

Several times a week,
    while up to their elbows in flour,
    women worked a bit of yeast
        into some soft dough
    and pondered a truth
        greater than rising bread.

. * . * .   . * . * .   . * . * .

Jesus seemed to have used
    a very long lecture
    with the crowds
        only a couple of times.   Lk 6; Jn 6

And, in one case,
    the results were disastrous!
He explained about himself
    as the Bread of Life
    for twenty-eight verses   Jn 6
        — intense, heavy expounding —

evidently ignoring
    the lack of readiness
    of at least some of his students.

He should have caught a message
    in verse sixty,
        when the squirming sundial watchers
        among the group
            began to fidget:

"This teaching is too hard. Who can listen to this?"

But he was so caught up
    in the importance of the thought
        that he charged ahead
        for another five verses!

And John notes rather bluntly
    in verse sixty-six:

        "Because of this, many of his followers turned back
            and would not go with him any more."

Long heavy lectures,
    with no breaks
    or change of activities,
        tend to run that way.
Maybe he tried it
    to show us what to avoid.

. * . * .   . * . * .   . * . * .

The "crowd" method
    which he seemed to rely on
    even more than pithy parables
    and long lectures
        was his own personal example.

Large Group Instruction — Crowds

The comforting townspeople of Naim
    were awestruck
        as they watched the Teacher
        console the grieving widow
            as none of them could do.   Lk 7:11-15
Thousands
    saw him concerned enough about their hunger
    to feed them.   Mt 14:13-21
They were impressed with his miracles
        to alleviate suffering,   Mt 8:5-13
    his fearlessness
        in dealing with hypocrisy,   Lk 12:1-3
    his gentleness
        with children   Mk 10:13-16
        and outcasts   Lk 5:12-16
        and sinners.   Jn 8:1-11

And, by his own heroic acceptance
    of his Father's Will
        in the Passion,
he taught all who wished to learn
    how to accept humiliation,
        physical and mental suffering,
        and even death.

. . .and for NOW   *. . . when we teach our "crowds"*

Re: Parables

With our instant mixes
    and twelve-lane asphalt freeways
        his parable principle still works,
        but not so well with yeast
        and fig trees.

How essential it is
    that teachers know thoroughly

what is truly "common and everyday"
in the lives of their students:

- about afterschool hangouts and hobbies
- about popular fads and fashions
- about sports and current t.v. and movie fare
- about momentary heroes and assorted "stars"

We can't create memorable parables
if we don't know
what's important
to our students.
Our current "yeast"
must be just as attention-grabbing
as his brand.

Re: Long Lectures
Don't!

Younger students,
and slower ones
have a very short attention span.
(Older ones
and brighter ones
aren't really much different.)

Long-winded teacher-explanations
are guaranteed
to create disciplinary problems
as one listener after another
reaches the end
of power-to-concentrate.

Ten minutes is a *LONG* time unless
a. the teacher is dynamic
b. the topic is novel
c. the students are enthralled

And if a. or b. or c.
    is missing
        the concentration time
        is proportionately shortened.

The seriousness
    of the disciplinary problems
    that will follow
        will depend upon the age
        and ingenuity
            of the students
        and the ability
        and agility
            of the teacher
                to change activities
                at the first glint of distraction
                    in the eye
                    of the first turned-off student.

If we must explain
    — and sometimes we must —
involve the students
    in "helping to explain",
        contributing as much as they know,
            with the teacher filling in gaps
            and adeptly stringing together
                the students' contributions
            into a logical framework.

The more they "own" the explanation,
    the less likely they are
        to "run out of listen".

Re: Personal Example

It's an old saying,
    but it's frighteningly true.
"Your actions shout so loudly that I can't hear your words."

What do we want our students to be?
honest? kind?
generous? truthful?
unselfish? joyous?
compassionate? obedient?
prayerful? courteous?

Are they seeing these things
as they WATCH US deal with
— their classmates?
— our families?
— the parish community?
— the rest of the faculty?
— the maintenance crew?

If they SEE what we mean
when we TELL them,
there's a 50/50 chance
they might choose to live
a Christian life.
If they don't SEE IN US,
what we TELL them,
the chances dwindle
a lot.

PART TWO

INDIVIDUALIZED INSTRUCTION

Paralytic

Part Two

INDIVIDUALIZED INSTRUCTION

Teachers who examine the encounters of Jesus with individuals will find themselves distracted by the many similarities between Jesus' students and their own. A closer meditative focus on a sampling will reveal that Jesus' techniques with every student matched the background, the readiness and the need of each one.

.*.*.*.   .*.*.*.   .*.*.*.

. . . the insecure
(Jn 5:1-18)

Thirty-eight years of doing nothing
      but lying on a mat
            would wipe out anybody's self-confidence.
            It could also provide plenty of support
                  for self-pity.

And the Teacher knew that.
Perhaps that's why Jesus' first words
      to the paralytic were:
            "Do you WANT to get well?"

The poor fellow's response
      held more than a trace of insecurity
      and a whimpering self-pity:

"Sir, I don't have anyone here
to put me in the pool
when the water is stirred up;
while I am trying to get in,
somebody else gets there first."

Jesus offered him no sympathy;
didn't even stretch out a hand
to help him up.
His words were a command for independence:
"Get up, pick up your mat, and walk."
You don't need anybody from now on.

And later when Jesus saw him again,
he reaffirmed that independence.

. . . and for NOW   . . . when we teach our "insecure ones"

— Never do for a student what she is capable of doing
for herself.

— The aim of teaching is to make the student independent
of the teacher.

— Create opportunities for the student to "prove
himself" to himself.

— Support with encouragement.

.*.*.*.   .*.*.*.   .*.*.*.

. . . the experimenter
(Mt 14:28-33)

Peter and the others were frightened enough
by the pre-dawn storm,

but the appearance of "the ghost"
　　　was just too much!

Only the sound of his voice
　　　and his usual message:
　　　　　　"Courage! It is I. Don't be afraid."
　　　put some degree of calm into them.

It was more than a relief to Peter.
It was a challenge.
　　　"Lord, if it is really you,
　　　　　　order me to come out
　　　　　　on the water
　　　　　　　　　to you."

And with one word: "Come!"
　　　permission was merged with encouragement.

Jesus gave Peter no warnings,
　　　no directions,
　　　no suggestions.
He merely kept an eye
　　　on the eager experimenter.

He was aware of Peter's fuzzy frame of faith;
　　　he certainly saw the feet sinking
　　　and the eyes stretched wide in fright.

　　　　　But he waited
　　　　　　　until his brave student
　　　　　　　called for help
　　　　　before he reached out to grab him.
　　　　　　　"Save me, Lord!"

Even as he hoisted Peter into the boat,
he offered a bit more encouragement:
　　　"Why did you doubt?"

WE could have done it
together.

. . . and for NOW   . . . when we teach our "experimenters"

— Create a setting for independent exploration.

— BE THERE, just in case.

— Build confidence by showing confidence.

— Be conscious of the ordinariness of mistakes
during early stages of learning
and share that information with students.
It lessens the sharpness of discouragement that
accompanies little failures.

. * . * . * .   . * . * . * .   . * . * . * .

. . . the eager
(Mk 10: 17-21; Mt 19:16-23)

The prospects for a thirteenth apostle
really looked promising.

The young fellow wanted to know
all about entering the Kingdom.
"What must I do to receive eternal life?"

He heard Jesus' answer
and felt encouraged;
but this student really wanted a challenge.

Commandments?
He'd been living those
— so, "What else do I need?"

Jesus was as eager in his answers
    as the young man was in his questions.

And the next two verses
    and especially *the space between them*
        hold some thoughts worth pondering.

Verse twenty-two tells us
    that the young man went away sad
    — disappointed when he realized
        that USING the new-found knowledge
        would alter his lifestyle.

The very next words:
    "Jesus looked around at his disciples and said . . ."
    tell us what Jesus *didn't* say.
He didn't call after the almost-apostle . . .
    "Could you sell at least *some* of your things?"
    "How about giving *part* of your money to the poor?"

He didn't compromise his message
    to gain a disciple.

  . . and for NOW   . . . when we teach our "eager ones"

    — Straightforward, honest questions
     deserve straightforward, honest answers.

    — No compromise with HIS message . . .
      That message is not to be watered down and adapted
      to lifestyles. On the contrary, lifestyles are to
      be shaped to fit the message.

             . * . * .   . * . * .   . * . * .

... the discouraged
(Lk 24:13-35)

Long faces,
slumped shoulders,
pace slowed by dejected spirits.
    It didn't take long to overtake them
    and walk along with them
        and teach them
            — though they didn't recognize him.

An all-knowing God asked:
    "What are you talking about?"
        and then paid very close attention
        as they detailed the cause of their misery.

ONLY AFTER he had drawn the problem
    from them
        did he explain in even greater detail
        everything necessary
            to bolster their courage
            and their faith.

He let himself be persuaded
    to stay for supper
    and some more talk.

And ONLY AFTER discouragement
    had released them
        did he leave them.

. . . and for NOW   *. . . when we teach our "discouraged ones"*

    — Recognize the signs of discouragement.

    — Create an opening for talk.

— Listen attentively to every detail.

— Encourage with facts.

— "Stay with them"
      until they've conquered discouragement.

.＊.＊.＊.   .＊.＊.＊.   .＊.＊.＊.

. . . the humiliated
(Jn 8:1-11)

A women in disgrace
    was brought before him.
She had been
    "caught in the very act of adultery"
    (evidently by self-righteous peeping-toms).

Her shocked accusers
    were horrified by the scandal.

And the woman,
    not only obviously aware of her shame,
    but abandoned by her family,
        her friends,
        and especially by her lover,
    silently faced the inevitability
    of being stoned.

And what did he do about it all?

He really seemed to ignore her
    until he had cleverly dispersed
    her accusers.

Only then did he quietly speak to her.
He gave her no sermon
— she didn't need it.
She was fully conscious of her guilt.

A gentle, ''Well then, I do not condemn you either.
Go, but do not sin again.''
was sufficient.

. . . and for NOW   *. . . when we teach our "humiliated ones"*

— Recall the purpose of correction:
to instruct,
to lead to self-control,
to enable the student to begin positive attitudes
and actions.

— Correct in private; if the offense was public, others
need only be aware that correction is being made.

— Speak in quiet, gentle tones.

— Never correct to get even with the offender.

. * . * . * .   . * . * . * .   . * . * . * .

. . . the masked
(Jn 4:1-30)

Jesus sat in the noonday sun
at Jacob's well
waiting for the woman
who wore a mask of indifference.

Had she been as nonchalant
    as she tried to appear,
She would have come to the well
    in the morning
        when the other village women
        collected to draw water
        and exchange local gossip.

At noon, the well was deserted.
No cold stares.
No accusing, hissing whispers
    carefully planted within earshot.

She didn't seem embarrassed
    to be addressed by a strange man,
    or at a loss for words
        in conversing with him.
That, evidently, had never been much of a problem
        for her.

He first asked her for a drink of water;
    and, in what must have sounded
        like useless banter to her,
            Jesus gradually led her unwittingly
            to ask him for Living Water.

And with one more slight turn of words,
    he asked her to call her husband.

His comment at her:
    "I don't have a husband,"
    was the perfect response
        for her.
            Which one?

No accusations,
no humiliating words,
only praise for the single element
    of good in her
       — her truthfulness.

He COMMENDS her for her truthfulness.

    "You are right when you say
        you don't have a husband. . .
    . . .You have told me the truth."

It's interesting to note
    that as she quickly changed the subject
    to a discussion on the best place to worship,
        Jesus didn't bring her attention back
        to her questionable lifestyle.
            No point in beating in the lesson
            when it's obviously been caught
            and flung away in shame.

He followed her lead
    and instructed her in worship,
    lifting her spiritually
        to a level she must have craved.

What a magnificent moment of learning!

This brazen, adulterous hussy
    became the first woman missionary
        as she forgot her water pot
        and ran to collect her neighbors
            to bring them
            to the Good News.

. . . and for NOW   *. . . when we teach our "masked ones"*

— A gentle request for a favor makes a good opener.
  "Give me a drink of water."   Jn 4:8

— Lead subtly to the truth.

— Search for the student's good quality,
  no matter how thoroughly covered.

— No need to nag and harp once the student is aware of
  the problem.

. * . * . * .   . * . * . * .   . * . * . * .

. . . the persevering searcher
(Mk 17:40-41, 47; 16:1-10; Lk 24:10-12; Jn 19:25; 20:1-18)

When He first came to know her
    her life was controlled by seven demons.   Lk 8:2
        And he put her life back
        into her own hands.

She chose to spend her time accompanying him
    as he preached the Good News
    through towns and villages,
        close to the source of her newfound peace.

The evangelists refer to her past,
    but spare her the embarrassment
    of describing it.
They become specific when they list her
    with the few women
    who kept vigil with his mother
        at the foot of his cross   Jn 19:25
        and before his newly sealed tomb   Mk 15:47
        on that Sabbath eve.

Mary Magdalene
    — listed not as having done something
        but as having been somewhere
    — moved from being to action
        when the moment called for it.

Every time she is mentioned with a group
    her name appears first —
    — indication of leadership?
    — distraught organizer
        of the Easter Morning grave visit,   Mk 16:1-4
            who remembered to bring spices to anoint him
            but overlooked the detail about moving the stone
    — woman with a single purpose:
        not to be separated
        from the source of her strength
            and her peace.

She was unbelievably persevering
    — despite the apparently superfluous message
        of the inconsequential angels
        who simply told her what she could see:
            "He is not here!"   Lk 24:6
    — despite the off-handed reception
        she received from his unbelieving
        and slow-moving disciples,
    — through the frantic search she started on her own
        to find Him
        when her discovery was doubted,
    — through the agonizing tears of grief
        and another frustrating encounter with angels
        who only asked her questions
            rather than answer
                the only one that mattered:
                    Where have they put him?
    — through the last encounter with the Gardener!

And how does he treat her?

He commissions her
    to deliver the Good News of His Resurrection
      to His Twelve.   Jn 20:17

Another first!
    — a person with a past
        commissioned to herald the future
          "I go back up to Him
             who is my Father and your Father
             my God and your God."
    — a persevering woman
        sent to proclaim His Message
        to the bewildered ones
          who would be his first Bishops.

He isn't bothered by protocol.
He ignores "tradition".

He commissions the person
    — for who she is
    — for what she has become
    — for her ability to get things done
    — for the potential he sees in her

The evangelists never mention her again.
No need to.

. . . and for NOW   *. . . when we teach our "persevering ones"*

    — Do we appreciate those
      who won't let the question drop until they understand
        — or do we find them annoying
          and tease them into satisfaction
            with surface knowledge?

— Do we open new avenues of exploration
    for their inquisitive minds
        — or do we become aggravated at their restlessness
           when we offer them conformity
              with how we've "always" done it?

— Do we meet students where they are
        — or where we wish they were,
           or where last year's class was "by now"?

— Do we reward the leadership and creativity
    that take our students beyond what we are capable of
        — or is there a greenish tint
           to our reluctant attempt to encourage
              critical thinking and independence?

He encouraged independence and leadership
    in all his students
        for he was leaving His message
           for future generations in their hands.

And if our message TODAY is still his,
    should we do less?

      . * . * .   . * . * .   . * . * .

. . . the unpopular, the unaccepted
(Mt 8:1-4; Mk 1:40-45; Lk 5:12-16)

He was unwanted
    shunned by his peers,
        untouchable — a leper;
his request, a simple:
    "Sir, if you want to, you can make me clean!"

The response of the concerned Teacher
    must have stunned the observers:
        he "reached out and *touched* him."

        He touched the untouchable!
        "I do want to . . . Be clean."

He further directed the man
    to fulfill the prescription of the Law
    "to prove to everyone that you are now clean."

The cleansed man needed
    not only to know that he was healthy
    but to regain acceptance
        by his family and his friends.

. . . *and for NOW*   *. . . when we teach our "untouchables"*

    — Our untouchables include:
        those with limited talents and intelligence,
        the grubby,
        the uncoordinated,
        those shunned because of handicaps,
        the unloved,
        the in-group's outsiders

    — "Touch them" in the presence of their peers —
        — by recognizing the worth of their ideas,
        — by seeking out their opinion and acting on it,
        — by appointing them to jobs which indicate
            YOUR RESPECT for their ability

    — Any student's self-acceptance hinges greatly
        on the acceptance received from both
        peers and significant adults.

.　*　.　*　.　　　　*　.　*　.　　　　.　*　.　*　.

Nicodemus

. . . the gifted
(Jn 3:1-12)

He had been studying the Teacher.

Nicodemus had thought profoundly enough
about the Teacher's message
to be filled with questions.
No surface information
could furnish answers;
no quick response could satisfy.

He was also on the verge
of breaking away
from peer pressure.

He needed time,
and privacy,
and individualized attention
— all needs of the gifted.

So he approached the Teacher
in the privacy provided by darkness
— 'after class'.

And the Teacher gave him time
and undivided attention.
He answered questions
and expanded the lesson as much
as THIS mind could handle.

. . . and for NOW   *. . . when we teach our "gifted ones"*

— Be alert for the 'after class' needs of students.

— Be conscious of eager students who,
    influenced by the need of acceptance
      by peers who are average,
    shy away from appearing interested in learning.

— Stretch a mind as far as it wants to expand.

— Know that the most important results of instruction
    are not evident at the close of a single lesson.
      (Jn 7:50; 19:39)

         . * . * . * .   . * . * . * .   . * . * . * .

. . . the crafty
    (Lk 19:1-9)

Luke tells us quite a lot
    about Zacchaeus
      in the first few verses of Chapter 19.

He was rich,
    curious,
      short,
        inventive,
          agile.
            — in that order.

    Only his occupation
      would have made him suspect.

Tax collectors weren't known for honesty.
    Craftiness, yes.
    Honesty, no.

He must have felt important,
    since Jesus met his need to be recognized
      first by calling Zacchaeus by name

and then by inviting himself
to be a guest
in the flustered man's home.

It's interesting to note:
it was the man's neighbors
who pointed out his sinfulness,
not the all-knowing Jesus.

And the addled Zacchaeus
responded to the Teacher
by announcing his sudden intention
of splitting his belongings with the poor,
and, just in case
of some forgotten moment of deception,
of repaying four-fold
anybody he'd cheated.

A spur-of-the-moment decision
to make restitution
BEFORE being accused of dishonesty
might indicate a troubled conscience.

And how did the Teacher respond?

He rejoiced at the conversion.
No: "It's about time, Zacchaeus!"
No penance given;
just rejoicing.

"Salvation has come to this house today;
this man also is a descendant of Abraham
For the Son of Man came
to seek
and to save
the lost."

. . . and for NOW   *. . . when we teach our "crafty ones"*

— All students need recognition — assurance that
others are aware of their personal worth and dignity.

— Learn students' names as soon as possible.
This says to each one:
"You're important and special to me."

— Praise students for their improvement, their effort.
Actual achievement will follow soon after.

— A thought:
No mention is made in Scripture about how lasting
Zacchaeus' conversion was. "Zacchaeus people" seem to
be quick to admit mistakes and promise amendment
— but perhaps just as quick to forget the whole
thing.

BUT JESUS REACHED OUT WITH AN OPPORTUNITY,
WITHOUT SCHEDULING A POST-TEST.
He believed in each student.

.*.*.*.   .*.*.*.   .*.*.*.

. . . the shy
(Mk 5:25-34; Lk 8:43-48)

Nothing distinctive marked
the woman's appearance.

Physically, she was weak
from twelve years of hemorrhaging.
Financially, she was poor,
having spent all she had
in search of doctors and cures.

In desperation
    she had joined the throng
        of believers
        and curiosity seekers
            who accompanied the Teacher
        on the way to the wake
        of a little girl.

Only the woman's desire to be healed
and her confidence in
    the power
    of the Teacher
        were strong.

In her timidity,
    she managed to edge her way
    close enough to touch the tip of his cloak
        and then to slip back into the crowd
            as she became aware of a sense
            of physical strength
            and wholeness
                surging through her body.

This model of shyness and fearfulness
    escaped the notice of everybody
        except Jesus,
        who turned instantly
            searching the crowd for her.

When the woman became aware of her discovery
    she stammered out what she had done.

Jesus respected her shyness.
By keeping his response short
    he did not prolong her moment
        in the spotlight.

He simply encouraged her
    "... YOUR FAITH has made you well."

... and for NOW   *... when we teach our "shy ones"*

— Seek them out.

— Offer gentle encouragement.

— Avoid limelight situations which tend to embarrass.

— Recognize that some students work best
    in settings away from footlights and fanfare.
    And every production IS DEPENDENT
    upon the writers and producers,
    the costume designers
    and the directors of lighting and stage sets
    — whom the audience never sees.

PART THREE

HIS HOMEROOM

Jesus, Apostles

Part Three

HIS HOMEROOM

Fortunate are the teachers
of the self-contained classroom
and those who have a homeroom.
Jesus, the Master Teacher also could say:
"So did I!"

Possibly
his contacts with the many individuals
who remain unnamed by the evangelists
were once-in-a-lifetime meetings;
and those in the crowds
probably had only a few personal encounters
with the Teacher.
In each instance
Jesus was gentle
or firm,
as the situation demanded.

With his apostles
it was an entirely different matter.
He was with them daily
as is a teacher with a class.

Surely there must have been
— good days
and bad ones

— occasions when the group was in high spirits
　　and sometimes low
— times of seriousness
　　and times of humor.

He was molding, guiding, forming them.

They were being prepared to continue his work,
　　although they didn't seem to understand that
　　　　until the last few days of their schooling.
They needed praise,
　　　　encouragement,
　　　　　　correction,
　　　　　　　　challenges,
　　　　　　　　　　sympathy.
And he provided for all their needs.

The variety among his apostles
　　in personality,
　　in ability,
　　and in cooperation with the Master
　　　　give any teacher inspiration and direction.

From the very beginning
　　he set about
　　to leave the mark of his philosophy
　　　　firmly imbedded in their hearts.

As early as the ninth chapter
　　of Matthew
he tried to instill in them
　　HIS LOVE OF HIS MISSION.

　　　　"There is a large harvest,
　　　　　　but few workers to gather it in.

Pray to the owner of the harvest
that he will send out workers
to gather in his harvest.''   Mt 9:37-38

But he wasn't waiting around
for somebody else to do the job.
He told Peter and the others:

"We must go on to the other villages around here.
I have to preach in them also,
because that is why I came.''   Mk 1:38

He went into great detail
about what it meant
to *belong* to this homeroom;
clear unmistakable directions
for a challenging future
if they chose to stay with him,
with no apologies
for the difficulties entailed.

And his students reached for the challenge
because they saw a perfect example
in the Teacher.   Mt 10:5-15; Mk 6:7-11; Lk 9:1-5

During his three years with them
he developed new concepts:
about loving one's enemies,   Mt 5:43-48
about a new view of the Sabbath,   Mt 12:1-8
about a unique form of prayer.   Mt 6:9-13

He gave them ample opportunities
to practice and apply those lessons
under his close supervision.

He created a variety of learning experiences
that they never forgot.

Consider what the Twelve must have learned when . . .

. . .he sent them on surprising errands	Lk 19:28-36; 22:7-13
. . .he posed problems to challenge them	Jn 6:5-6
. . .he demonstrated lessons	Jn 13:4-17
. . .he warned them about evil influence	Mt 23:1-12
. . .he puzzled them	Jn 20:3-10; Mk 4:34
. . .he gave them advice	Lk 12:1-5
. . .he corrected them	Jn 12:4-8; Mk 8:33
. . .he grouped them, apparently without causing jealousy among them	Mk 5:37; 9:2; 14:33
. . .he gave orders	Lk 9:1-6
. . .he forced them to take a stand on issues	Mk 8:27-30
. . .he asked for their assistance, support	Mt 26:36-38
. . .he defended them	Mt 12:1-8; Jn 18:7-9
. . .he responded to their petitions	Lk 11:1-13
. . .he scolded them	Mk 16:14
. . .he teased them into learning	Lk 24:13-35
. . .he aroused their curiosity	Mk 13:1-6ff.
. . .he prepared them gently for a difficult situation	Jn 13:21-30
. . .he gave them extra help with hard lessons	Lk 8:9-18; Mk 4:34
. . .he introduced them to prayer by his own example	Mk 1:35-38
. . .he made them come to grips with what they believed	Lk 9:18-20
. . .he expressed impatience with their slowness	Mk 8:14-21
(. . .but he was dealing with adults, not children)	
. . .he gave them a chance to "save face"	Jn 21:15-19
. . .he affirmed them for going beyond what was taught	Mt 16:17
. . .he took them on field trips	
— always to strengthen their faith	
— to Cana for a wedding feast	Jn 2:1-12
— on a walk to find a fig tree	Mk 11:12-14, 20-24
— to Bethany for a resurrection	Jn 11:11-44
— to Mt. Tabor for a meeting	Mk 9:2-10

. * . * . *.   . * . * . *.   . * . * . *.

Not only did he explain his mission,
 he empowered the Twelve with his authority
  to do what he could do:
   ". . .drive out evil spirits
   and to heal every disease and every sickness." Mt 10:1

He was mindful of the purpose of *all* teaching
 — to develop independence in the student.

Jesus *earned* the respect and trust of the Twelve.
They obviously were in awe of him.
 But in their early attempts
  to use his healing power
  which he had shared with them,
   they weren't always successful.

It was evidently with great relief
 that Jesus was spotted by the man
  whose son was possessed by an evil spirit.

Some of the Teacher's disciples
 had made an unsuccessful attempt
 to heal the troubled boy,
  and that had resulted
   in drawing a curious crowd
   to witness the argument
    that ensued between the frustrated disciples
    and the boy's disappointed father.

Jesus took command of the situation
 and for the next eight verses
 Mark omits any reference
  to the disciples watching the scene
  intently from the sidelines.
Mark refers to them again
 "after Jesus had gone indoors".

Only then did they ask him in private,
    "Why couldn't we drive the spirit out?"

THEY referred to the failure,
    not HE.
They felt comfortable
    and secure in his presence.
They knew he would not ridicule their efforts
    and their failure;
        he would simply give them further instruction:
        "Only prayer can drive this kind out, nothing else can."

                                                      Mk 9:14-28

. * . * . *.   . * . * . *.   . * . * . *.

On another occasion
    the disciples had just heard Jesus
        — in one packed sentence —
            predict the destruction of the Temple:

        ". . .Not a single stone will be left in its place;
            every one of them will be thrown down."   Mk 13:2

For Peter, Andrew, James, and John
    such an answer needed expansion;
        so they "came to him in private.
          'Tell us when this will be. . .' "

His consistency of manner
    made them certain
        that they would be answered at length,
            and they were right.   Mk 13:5-37

. * . *.   . * . * .   . * . *.

Eager
but not always sharp!

They had just witnessed some Pharisees
    attempting to entrap the Teacher
        and perhaps
        it had unnerved them somewhat
            — too distracted to remember
                to pack enough lunch
                    for the boat trip across the lake.

Then they mistook
    his reminder about "yeast of Pharisees"
    to be a reprimand
        about their forgetfulness.

Embarrassment has a way
    of compounding troubles
        — and they were embarrassed.

And HE must have been a bit edgy
    — "Don't you know or understand yet?
        Are your minds so dull?"

But he did a quick review
    reminding them
    of the bread-miracles
        they had recently witnessed.
            "How is it that you don't understand
            that I was not talking to you
                about bread?"

Matthew's verse twelve begins with
    "THEN the disciples understood. . ."   Mt 16:1-12; Mk 8:11-21

. . .Development: no response.
. . .Some more development: misunderstanding.
. . .Review and drill: *maybe* a little understanding.

It was that way when he taught.
Why should it be different for us?

. * . * . * .   * . * . * .   . * . * . * .

He was able
    to create a wonderful rapport
      with his homeroom.

He loved and respected them
    and they obviously knew that.
      They responded with love and respect.
Evidently they felt
    comfortable enough with him
    to speak in a very familiar fashion
      without his taking it amiss.

. . .They must have been wild in panic
    as the crashing waves began to drench them
    and fill their wind-whipped boat.
To add to their distress
    the Master slept soundly in the stern,
    his head cushioned comfortably
      on a pillow!

The awakening
    must have been a jolting one
    as they gave a distraught shout:
      "Teacher, don't you care
      that we are about to die?"

He "*commanded*" the wind,
    but he "*said*" to his disciples,
        probably in a tone
        that matched the ensuing calm:

        "Why are you frightened?
        Are you still without faith?"   Mk 4:37-40

   . * . * . * .   . * . * . * .   . * . * . * .

They seemed to be protective of him.

. . .His disciples were good
    at reminding the Teacher
        lest he forget
        his usual schedule.

When the crowds began to assemble,
    Simon and the others spent time
    searching for him
        and they found him
        in his "lonely place" of prayer.
They seemed to ignore
what he'd been doing.
        "Everyone is looking for you," they told him.   Mk 1:36

. . .And after some stiff words
    to the Pharisees,
        the Teacher heard a friendly cautioning
        from his twelve:
            "Do you know
            the Pharisees had their feelings hurt
                by what you said?"   Mt 15:12

. . .As crowds of people
 swarmed about him on the way
  to Jairus' house,
   he sensed the touch
   of someone in need
    of his healing power.

 "Who touched my clothes?" he asked.

 His disciples had the answer:

 "You see how the people are crowding you;
  why do you ask who touched you?"

His response?

 "But Jesus kept looking around
  to see who had done it."

NO REBUKE FOR WORDS
 THAT AN INSECURE TEACHER
  MIGHT HAVE CONSIDERED RUDE
   OR DISRESPECTFUL.   Mk 5:29-32

   . * . *. *. . *. *. *. . *. *. *.

Only once,
 when Simon's suggestion
 was opposed to principle
  did he hear
   the Teacher's rebuke.   Mk 8:33

   . * . *. *. . *. *. *. . *. *. *.

And once,
 "They did not understand
 what this teaching meant,

but they were afraid to ask him.''
Maybe they were afraid
because they sensed the answer. Mk 9:32

. * . * . *. . * . * . *. . * . * . *.

Jesus concluded
his disciples' three years of instruction
with a significant supper.

He reviewed the major concepts
he had taught.
And he summarized his philosophy
into a new commandment
of love. Jn 13:34

He even designated
the insignia of his school:
that his disciples
have love for one another. Jn 13:35

. . . and for NOW *. . . when we teach our homeroom*

— When there is mutual love and respect
between teacher and students
openness can grow.
Tone of voice, words,
even interpretation of motives
become funneled
through understanding and trust.

But the teacher who waits for students' respect
waits in vain.
Students have a way of reflecting
the respect given them by the teacher.

PART FOUR

EDUCATIONAL TIPS FROM
THE MASTER

A Cure Of The Blind

Part Four

EDUCATIONAL TIPS FROM THE MASTER

No HOW-TO book for teachers is complete without a section on miscellaneous topics that are too scattered, and independently too insignificant to merit a whole chapter on each one. But any teacher on any level recognizes the Significance of the Insignificant in dealing with students, equipment, organization. In teaching it's hard to find the insignificant. So the topics here are listed alphabetically to eliminate the need of listing them in the order of "importance".

Audio-Visual Aids, effective use of

Jesus never used an overhead projector
    or showed a filmstrip.
For audio-visual aids
    he made the best use
        of available objects,
        produced at the most strategic moment.
He wasn't limited
    to what he could list
    on a requisition blank,
        filled out in duplicate
        and submitted by 2:15 p.m.
        on Tuesday.

.*.*.*.   .*.*.*.   .*.*.*.

They set out to trap him about the justice of paying taxes. . .
   "Show me the coin to pay the tax."
      And they dug out a coin from a purse
      and studied it meticulously
         as if they'd never seen it before.
   "Whose face and name are these?"

     . . .and he made his point.   Mt 22:15-22

    . * . * . * .   . * . * . * .   . * . * . * .

To settle an argument among his more ambitious disciples
   "He took a child, stood him by his side. . ."
   "He took a child and made him stand in front of him
      . . .put his arms around him. . ."

      (Was the child squirming?
            anxious to get back to his play?
            nervous about being the center of attention?)

   "He called a child, had him stand in front of them. . ."

     . . .and taught them about simplicity and innocence and
        the dignity of children.   Lk 9:46-48; Mk 9:36; Mt 18:2

    . * . * . * .   . * . * . * .   . * . * . * .

A barren fig tree
along the road from Bethany
   withered up at the Teacher's command;
and lessons were learned
   about Faith,
   about prayer.   Mk 11:12-14, 20-24

    . * . * . * .   . * . * . * .   . * . * . * .

He needed something
    a bit dramatic
        to build up the disciples' trust
           in him.
And a storm was the perfect audio-visual aid.   Mk 4:35-41

. . .Sometimes a touch of drama
    does the same service for us.

       . * . * . * .   . * . * . * .   . * . * .

He was watching people
    dropping their temple tax
        into the treasury
when he noticed her.

The poor widow,
her two copper coins
and her motive
    were perfect for his lesson
        on generous giving,
        "So he called his disciples together and said. . ."

And as they were leaving the temple
his disciples called his attention
    to the building
    and its wonderful stones
        and he taught them a second lesson.   Mk 12:41-44; 13:1-2

       . * . * .   . * . * .   . * . * .

The Teacher met the man-born-blind
    somewhere along the dusty road,
        — hardly the place
           to find sophisticated equipment
           and learning aids.

But he managed to make
    a little healing mud
        from his own spittle
        and the ground,
and taught his disciples
    a lesson about the Light of the World.

A budget-of-nothing
    can produce creative adaptations!   Jn 9:6-7

. * . * . * .   . * . * . * .   . * . * . * .

He simply used water,
    plain water
    and some nearby jars
        to begin to establish
        his credibility as Teacher;

    and some available bread
    and fish
        to teach a lesson on caring.   Jn 2:1-12; 6:1-15

He borrowed 2000 pigs
    to rid a man of some demons.   Mk 5:1-19

The ground
and his finger
    substituted for chalkboard and chalk.
Primitive, but effective
    in clearing the area
    of some trouble-makers.   Jn 8:1-11

A towel
and a washbasin of water
    were all he needed
    to teach the Twelve
        an attitude of service.

"I have set an example for you
　　. . .how happy you will be
　　　　if you put it into practice." Jn 13:4-17

And he used Thomas' hand
　　to teach *us* a lesson:
　　　　"How happy are those who believe
　　　　　　without seeing me!" Jn 20:27-29

　　　　　　.*.*.*.　　.*.*.*.　　.*.*.*.

Although he made use
　　of many objects;
mostly,
　　　　he used the touch of his hand
　　　　and gentle, encouraging words
　　　　　　to heal the diseases of bodies
　　　　　　and souls.

. . .*and for NOW*　　　　　　*. . .when we use our visual aids*

In this time of projectors,
　　　　　　computers,
　　　　　　and catalogs of technological inventions
　　　　　　　　and advancements,
　　　　maybe his message is:

Effective use of a little can result in tremendous learning.

The Teacher started
　　by setting the GOAL of the lesson,
　　　　then he selected his aids
　　　　— never the reverse order.

Jesus, children

Maybe the greater lessons we teach
    have to do with attitudes and values,
        not knowledge and skills.
Should we rethink our goals?
            our priorities?

Children, attitudes toward

Jesus apparently never provided
    any special classes
        to teach his message to children.

He blessed them;
he put one in the midst
    of his ambitious apostles,
and he referred to them often enough
    to give a good indication
        of his attitude toward them.

As his apostles sheepishly looked
    at the child he had placed in front of them,
the Teacher spoke very forcefully:
    "Unless you CHANGE AND BECOME LIKE CHILDREN
    you will never enter the Kingdom of heaven.
        The greatest in the Kingdom of heaven
          is one who humbles himself
          and becomes like this child."   Mt 18:3-4

He seemed to equate humility
    with childlikeness.
And his words
    raised the dignity of every child
        to an astounding height.

             * . * . * .   . * . * .   . * . * .

Jesus is recorded as being angry twice:
  once with the money changers
    abusing his Father's house
  and once with his disciples
    as they scolded the people
      who brought their children
      (Luke calls them "babies")
        for his blessing.

He SPOKE to the disciples:

> "Let the children come to me, and do not stop them,
>   because the Kingdom of heaven
>   belongs to such as these."   Mk 10:15

But he BLESSED the children:

> "He took the children in his arms
>   placed his hands on each of them
>   and blessed them."   Mk 10:16

. * . * . *.   . * . * .   . * . * .

Matthew adds one more insight
into the Teacher's attitude toward children:

> "See that you don't despise
>   any of these little ones.
>   Their angels in heaven, I tell you,
>   are always in the presence of
>   my Father in heaven."   Mt 18:10

His view about those
    who would cause "little ones"
      to lose faith in Him

should make all teachers think seriously
about their personal example,
as well as how positively
and accurately
they deliver His message
to children and young people.

.*.*.*.   .*.*.*.   .*.*.*.

One last consideration
— perhaps we need to pass on a message
to the children we teach.

Maybe we should make them aware
of their responsibility
to show the adults in their lives
the kind of behavior and attitudes
that will result
in "possessing heaven".

Correcting Students

A significant part of teaching
is correcting students.
Jesus used several techniques
to accomplish this task.

— He *told a story* about the first and last places to
correct some proud students   Lk 14:7-14

— He *gave a warning* to the overly confident Peter
"Remember this! Before the rooster crows. . ."   Mt 26:31-35

— A *look of reproof* was enough to make Peter remember
the warning he had ignored earlier.

"The Lord turned around and looked straight at Peter
and Peter remembered the Lord's words. . ."   Lk 22:61-72

— He *gave a short pointed talk*
to set his apostles straight
when they became angry
at James and John
for making premature bids
for places of honor in his kingdom.   Mt 20:24-28

— He *gave a sharp command* to Peter:
". . .Put your sword back in its place!"   Jn 18:11

. . .*and for NOW*   . . .*when we correct our students*

It seems that the only times
he used insulting, harsh words
and dramatic, angry actions
were when he was dealing
with HEARTS HARDENED WITH YEARS OF ADULT CHOICES
of hypocrisy and greed,
of pride and selfishness
— the scribes, the pharisees,
the money-changers.

For those of us
who deal with children,
youth,
and young adults
this manner of correction
is totally out of place.

Our students may be awkward,
thoughtless,
inconsiderate,
clumsy,

foolish,
        annoying,
                aggravating
                        and even irritating at times.

If they APPEAR TO BE HARDENED,
        maybe we ought to look at the adult influences in their
        lives. . .

                — adult-produced films and television programs
                — adult-produced books and magazines
                — adult-produced drugs and alcohol
                — adult example all around them.

But when we correct our students
        the gentle,
                forgiving,
                loving methods of the Master should be evident.

Avoid using the techniques Jesus saved for hardened adults.

Directions, giving of

Universally, teachers fret
        over the inability of students
                to follow directions.
Years after HIS directions were given
and followed
        three of the evangelists
        were able to record them.

Excellent record!

Maybe the clarity did it:

Directions

"Go to the village there ahead of you;
    as you go in you will find a colt tied up
        that has never been ridden.
Untie it and bring it here.
If someone asks you 'Why are you untying it?'
    tell him 'The Master needs it.'

"THEY WENT ON THEIR WAY AND FOUND EVERYTHING
    JUST AS JESUS HAD TOLD THEM."   Lk 19:29-32

. * . * . * .   . * . * . * .   . * . * . * .

He was just as precise
    in his directions
    about the Passover meal
        when Peter and John asked him:

        "Where do you want us to get it ready?"

Instead of answering with an address
    Jesus sent them to find
    and follow a man doing "women's work"
        — carrying a water jar.

In those pre-feminist times
    such a man
    probably would have been quite conspicuous!

And as usual
    they "found everything just as Jesus had told them."   Lk 22:10-12

. * . * .   . * . * .   . * . * .

Earlier,
he had been just as explicit

in his directions
    when he organized the Twelve
    for their first teaching experience.

He was very precise
    in listing everything
    they *shouldn't* take on the journey,
        possibly because it was just the opposite
        of what they'd expect
            an itinerant teacher to pack:
            no bread,
              no bag,
                no extra shirt,
                no money,
                    no walking stick.

                And no shoes — just wear sandals.

However
Mark took a little liberty
    with the listing.
He included the walking stick
    with the sandals.
But Mark hadn't been there
    when the directions were given;
        he simply recorded
        what Peter remembered
            about the occasion.

So much for expecting exact directions
    to be repeated accurately
        by a student
        for latecomers!   Mt 10:9-10; Mk 6:7-9; Lk 9:3

          . * . * .   . * . * .   . * . * .

Even in his miracle working he was very definite:

". . .stretch out your hand."	Mt 12:13
"Get up, pick up your mat and go home."	Mk 2:11
"Go and let the priests examine you."	Lk 17:14

And the directions were always followed
with exciting and astounding results.

. *. *. *.   . *. *. *.   . *. *. *.

It seems
that the only times
people ignored his directions
were when the newly-cured were warned
to tell no one what had happened!   Lk 5:14; Mk 7:36; Mt 9:30

. . .and for NOW   . . .when we give directions

— Directions need to be clear, to the point.

— Maybe we need to rethink
the IMPORTANCE of all the directions we give.
How much is really necessary
to achieve the major goal of the lesson?

— Do our students tend to get
so entangled in the minutia of trifling, detailed directions
and irrelevant rules of procedure
that they lose sight of the learning before them?

Learning Settings, choosing the best

"I can't teach near the music room."
"I'd prefer a smaller room at the east end
of the old wing."
"It's useless to try to teach anything after Easter

. . .after two in the afternoon
   . . .the week before Christmas
      . . .with more than twenty-eight in the class.''

We are so conscious
   of when and where we can or can't teach.
We do our best
   when the place and the time are perfect.

Maybe we should glance at the settings
   when Jesus ''did his best''.

To cite a few. . .

   . . .He managed to explain the beatitudes
      sitting on a hillside
         surrounded by thousands.   Mt 5:1-12

   . . .He sat at the lakeside until he felt too crowded;
      then he created a bit of distance
         by moving to a boat
         where he taught the people
            standing in the wet sand,
            listening to the parables
               he would explain later to his Twelve.   Mt 13:1-3

   . . .He taught with just as much authority
      in the house of a tax collector   Mt 9:9-13
         as he did in the synagogue.   Mk 1:21-22

   . . .He taught in the towns   Mt 11:1
      and in lonely places;   Mk 1:45
         in a wheat field while his disciples snacked,   Mt 12:1-8
         and ON the water
            while one of them sank.   Mt 14:28-33

. . .In the Temple
    he was surrounded by goats and doves and money changers
                                     Jn 2:13-20

    in the Garden of Olives,
        by drowsing friends
            — and he kept doing his best.   Mk 14:37-42

. . .He taught at a wedding reception
    after the guests had depleted the refreshments.   Jn 2:1-12

. . .The Upper Room was the center
    of some of his most intense instruction
        with his homeroom group
            both before and after his resurrection.
                           Jn 13-17; 20:19-29

. . .He taught at the grave of a dear friend   Jn 11:38-44
    and at the home of an enemy.   Lk 7:36-50

. . .He taught Nicodemus late at night,   Jn 3:1-21
    and Mary Magdalene as the sunlight
        first touched his own tomb.   Jn 20:11-18

. . .Even on the cross, he taught
    — as he was laying down his life
        for all those who would ever learn from him,
        and for those who wouldn't.
                    Lk 23:34, 39-43; Jn 19:26-30

His best time
    seemed to have been
        all the time;
the best place,
    any place.

Perhaps the difference
    between his *best* setting and ours
        is the VIEW OF THE MISSION.

He knew that each teaching moment
    would be the only moment for some student.
He taught with an urgency
    because he had only three short years
        to accomplish his task.

So every moment,
    in every setting
        became A TEACHING MOMENT.

And is it not the same with us?
Only we usually have not three years,
    but only one year
        with a group of students.

Ought not our teaching
    reflect that same urgency?
        that same dynamism?

Life-Changing Lessons

The most important lessons
    Jesus wanted to instill
        were taught again and again
        with all the variety he could muster.

He taught in layers. . . gradually. . .
    . . .to awaken awareness
        he demonstrated

. . .to instruct for understanding
    he talked about it
    he gave them opportunities for practice
    he explained in detail

. . .to inspire for total acceptance
    he showed them how to live the truth
    he expected mastery
        — according to personal ability

He used this system for concepts he valued most.

. . .for PRAYER

Early in the disciples' education
    they evidently missed the point entirely.

Although they were aware of the Teacher's habit
    of seeking out lonely places   Lk 5:16
    in the only uninterrupted time he had
        — late at night
            through the early morning hours —
    they didn't hesitate
    to charge in to announce visitors.   Mk 1:35

Perhaps they'd learned to take his prayer for granted
    since ". . .on the Sabbath day
    he went *as usual* to the synagogue."   Lk 4:16-27

They gradually must have become aware
    of the necessity of prayer
    as they observed the value he placed upon it.

    He prayed at meals.   Mt 14:19; Mk 14:22
    His prayer seemed to be in proportion

to the event he prayed about
— forty days of it
before beginning his public teaching
Mt 4:1-11; Mk 1:12-13; Lk 4:1-13

— a night of it before he chose his disciples
Lk 6:12-13

They must have been surprised to hear him
— direct them to pray for their persecutors   Mt 5:44-45
— insist that they pray
in the privacy of their own room
and in few words   Mt 6:5-13
— encourage them to imitate
the persistent widow and the tax collector
— tell them to pray always and never get discouraged
Lk 18:1-8; 10-14
— encourage them to gather in little groups for prayer
Mt 18:19-20

They must have noted
the powerful answers to his prayer
— after his baptism   Lk 3:21-22
— when Peter, James, and John
went up a hill with him to pray
and discovered Moses and Elijah   Lk 9:28-36

And ''one time Jesus was praying
in a certain place.
WHEN HE FINISHED. . .''
— they'd finally realized what he was doing
— they'd seen enough, been inspired enough
to WANT TO KNOW how to pray.
And he taught them his prayer.   Lk 11:1-13

His final instruction was his example.
— praying to the Father for them
— while eleven of them watched intently
not really understanding   Jn 17:1-26

— praying to the Father for himself
    — while three of them
      spent a drowsy hour or so with him
          Mt 26:36-46; Mk 14:32-40; Lk 22:39-46

. . .for FORGIVENESS OF SINS

Although they'd seen him forgive the sins
    — of the paralyzed man   Lk 5:20
    — of the woman with the alabaster perfume jar   Lk 7:36-50

And they'd heard him preach forgiveness
    — even if the brothers came
      seven times in one day to apologize   Lk 17:3
    — even if Peter's hypothetical brother
      offended him another seven times,   Mt 18:21-35

How prepared were they
    for his own example of forgiveness. . .
      "Forgive them, Father!
      They don't know what they are doing. . ."?   Lk 23:34

How astounded to hear him
    empower them to continue his forgiving:
      "Receive the Holy Spirit.
      If you forgive men's sins, they are forgiven. . ."
          Jn 20:22-23

. . .for RESPECT FOR THE DIGNITY OF EVERY PERSON

He consoled the tax collectors
    and other outcasts who came to hear him.
      They saw themselves in his parables
      about the lost sheep,
        the lost coin,
        and the lost son.   Lk 15:1-32

And they must have been
a little flattered
    as they sheepishly heard their techniques
    described in the shrewd manager's dealings.   Lk 16:1-9

But they knew he respected them.
    Hadn't he already chosen one of them
    as his own disciple?
        Hadn't they attended the fine banquet
        Levi gave to celebrate his own calling?   Lk 5:27-32

And the same respect he'd shown
    to each questionable character
        — the woman caught in adultery   Jn 8:1-11
        — the tree-climbing tax collector   Lk 19:1-9
        — the woman possessed of seven demons   Lk 8:2

    . . .they saw again
        as he welcomed the thief to join him in paradise.   Lk 23:6

He LIVED his message before he taught it.
He expected his followers to do the same.

. . .about EARTHLY RICHES

They had seen him poor in things,
    yet rich in generosity with his time,
    his gift of miracles.
They probably weren't very surprised
    to hear him direct them:
        ". . .So don't be all upset,
            always concerned
            about what you will eat and drink.
        . . .Instead be concerned with his Kingdom
            and he will provide you with these things.

. . .Sell all your belongings
and give the money to the poor.'' Lk 12:29-33

.*.*.*. .*.*.*. .*.*.*.

BUT LESSON PLANS SHOULD BE RATHER RUBBERY. . .
. . .easily changed and adapted
according to the needs of the students
. . .so he often varied his procedure.

. . .He taught His beatitudes
before his disciples had had a chance
to see him live them; Mt 5:1-12
but demonstrations of proper procedures
followed by teacher-example
are also effective.

. . .He used this technique again Lk 9:23
when he told them
that one of the conditions of discipleship
was taking up a personal cross. Lk 14:27
And he said this
before his disciples
could have had any inkling
about His Cross.

. . .and for NOW . . .when we teach our life-changing lessons

— ''Layered'' teaching still works.
. . .Let them see the lesson
in the teacher's attitudes and actions
before they hear what they're supposed to be learning.

— *Awareness digs the hole for the foundation.*
— No value in testing at this point;
only the most perceptive students
may have grasped the lesson.

. . .For a life-changing idea to be absorbed
students need to examine it in a variety of ways,
to be immersed in it,
to practice it,
and have opportunities to live it
and see it lived.

— Instruction erects the scaffolding.
— Not much value in testing at this point;
probably only some of the students
may have caught the lesson,
with varying degrees of accuracy.

. . .*Total acceptance* of such an idea is usually gradual,
the significant change, imperceptible.
— Even the student doesn't realize
MASTERY has been achieved
until and unless the lesson is challenged,
sometimes years after the teaching.

— *Living the lesson brings the edifice to completion.*
— By the time the student is ready for testing
the period of learning may be months,
even decades in the past.
— long after the student has forgotten
the teacher's carefully prepared
lessons
and probably, even the teacher.

Member of a Staff

He worked well in departmentalized settings.
John the Baptist had taught
the readiness class in Christian Living.

Although Jesus took the beginners
and the advanced group,
    he held in highest esteem
    the person of John and his work.
Jesus' words to the Baptist's disciples
    certainly must have given John
        a sense of worth and accomplishment,
    and given his message
        credibility in the minds of his disciples.

    ". . .Remember this!
        John the Baptist is greater than
            any man who has ever lived. . ."   Mt 11:7-15

. . .and for NOW   *. . .when referring to "last year's teacher"*

   — Our students' previous teachers deserve our respect.
     If OUR message is to produce growth
     it must be seen by our students
        as worthwhile knowledge
         to *add to*
     what they have already acquired
        from former teachers.

   — Teamwork among our faculty and staff who respect one another
     will make a positive contribution to our students' education.

Parent-Teacher Conference

In a moment of parental pride
    (or possibly at the suggestion of her sons),
        Mrs. Zebedee approached Jesus
        in the one recorded parent-teacher conference.

She was polite about it,
    bowing before the Teacher;

Mother of James and John

and she wasn't the least bit hesitant
in answering
his: "What do you want?"

"*Promise* that these two sons of mine
will sit at your right and your left
when you are King."

A strong first word;
and not for only one son,
— but for both of them!

Jesus didn't answer "her";
he answered "them".
He addressed his remarks
to the students
in the presence of the mother:

"You don't know what you are asking for.
Can you drink the cup that I am about to drink?"   Mt 20:20-23

. . .*and for NOW*   . . .*at our parent-teacher conferences*

— Perhaps this technique
would put the focus on the trouble-spot
especially when stories
tend to develop many extra facets
and shades of meaning
as they get retold
in different settings
in the presence of different people.

Planning, long-ranged

Complex lessons
take more advanced planning
than simpler ones.

The Teacher had a way
of creating outstanding learning experiences.
The dramatic multiplication of loaves and fishes
and the generation of an instant-storm to calm   Mk 4:35-41
inspired wonder
and fanned the spark of Faith
within his apostles.

. * . * . * .   . * . * . * .   . * . * . * .

In another instance
Jesus had begun his preparation
for a strategic lesson
probably before his own birth!

The Teacher and his followers
had happened upon a blind man
along the way;
and, in passing,
the disciples had inquired
about the cause of the blindness.

Was it the man's sinfulness
or his parents'?

Jesus told them plainly
that nobody's sin
had anything to do
with the man's condition.

But the fourth and fifth words
of his next sentence
revealed some spectacular long-ranged planning.

"He is blind SO THAT God's power might be
seen at work in him."

Since birth
    this man had lived in darkness
       ". . .SO THAT God's power might be seen. . ."

How's that for preparing for a lesson!   Jn 9:1-5

. * . * . * .   . * . * . * .   . * . * . * .

On another occasion
Jesus deliberately waited for days
    before he responded to the summons
    to visit his sick friend Lazarus.

Again, the Teacher planned ahead
    for the most effective of lessons.   Jn 11:1-15

. . .and for NOW   *. . .when we plan*

   — The teacher's attitude toward the real goal of the lesson
      will determine how much time and effort
      will go into the preparation for it.

   — Although many effective lessons can be taught and learned
      in spontaneous settings
          we can't depend on spontaneity
          to provide for all lessons.

     We're likely to limit our students' opportunities
     to incidental learning
        if we don't make a conscious effort
           to plan strategically
           and well in advance.

September-June

In the "September of his teaching"
    it seems that
        Jesus did much demonstrating
        and explaining
            while his disciples
            were observing and asking questions.

By the "end of the first semester"
    his disciples were assisting him,
    being sent to use his power
        in his name.

And during his last six weeks with them
    he adjusted his methods again
        to meet their needs.

At the last supper
    he prayed with them
    and for them,
        he reviewed the highlights
            of all his teachings for them;
        he gave them final directions
            and prepared them
            to receive their next teacher:

        "The Helper, the Holy Spirit whom the Father
            will send in my name."   Jn 14:26

Then he put them through
    the most rigorous final examination
        from Thursday night
        until early Sunday morning,
            testing all they'd been taught by him.

AND THE TESTING RESULTS
WERE ENOUGH TO DISCOURAGE
ANY TEACHER
— One apparently failed.
— And of the other eleven,
all but one were too afraid
to be present for the exam!

But testing only indicates
how much more work
the teacher needs to do.

So, just look
at the forty-day remediation
he provided!

Faith must have been strengthened
and deepened;
hope, resurrected
with each of his encouraging appearances.

And they finally learned the meaning of his words:

"As I have loved you, so must you love one another."   Jn 13:34

. * . * .   . * . * .   . * . * .

It's obvious that three years
with him
had made a great difference
in the lives of the Twelve.

They "went back to Jerusalem
filled with great joy
and spent all their time
in the temple
giving thanks to God."   Lk 24:52-53

And "They gathered frequently
to pray as a group
together with the women,
and with Mary
the Mother of Jesus,
and his brothers."   Ac 1:14

They also chose Matthias to replace Judas.   Ac 1:26

Thus, for ten days they prepared themselves
for the Teacher's successor
who would teach them everything
and make them
"remember all that I have taught you."   Jn 14:26

. . .*And for NOW*   . . .*When we assess our teaching*

The true test of learning
certainly can't be determined
by a five point quiz
at the end of a forty minute lesson
or a four-page test
after a few weeks' study of a topic.

Learning
THAT MAKES A DIFFERENCE IN LIVES
must penetrate much deeper
than the surface information
skimmed from books
which coats the outer layers of the mind.

— What's the use of drilling verb tenses
and sentence sense and punctuation marks
if we haven't taught our students
how to communicate
in honesty, in truth, and in love?

— What's the purpose of having them
  speeding through country-capital associations
   if we haven't taught them
    to love, appreciate, and accept
     other cultures and peoples?

— What's the purpose of checking memorized prayers
  if we haven't taught them
  HOW TO pray?

— What's the use of teaching them
  to name every human bone and muscle
   if we haven't taught them to respect life
    in its every stage and form?

— What's the purpose of knowing
  every form of investment and means of profit
   if they don't know the relative value
    of all things material,
   if they aren't generous with what they have?

— What's the value of being able to recognize
  every major work of every notable artist and composer
   if they can't appreciate all forms of beauty
    and all effort exerted to produce it?

— What's the use of developing intellectual geniuses
  if we haven't taught them to be grateful,
   to be kind, to be respectful
   and helpful to those with lesser talents?

The real test of learning comes
  after the teacher and students
   are separated
    — not by bookshelves
     or classroom walls

> — but by the space of years,
>   and then by the gulf
>   between time and eternity.

What will our students be doing
    with their lives
        to improve
        their world?

Sense of Humor

Humor —
    quiet, gentle,
    sometimes seemingly tongue-in-cheek,
        but it was there.
The scenes bring a smile
    as we read the details
        recorded so perceptively by the evangelists.

                    .*.*.*.   .*.*.*.   .*.*.*.

He had "made his disciples get into the boat"
    and waved them off.
Then he dispersed the crowd
    and prayed into the night.

Before dawn,
    from the shore
    "he saw"
        that they were having a tough time
        rowing against the wind.
So "he came to them
    walking on the water"

and "HE WAS GOING TO PASS THEM BY
  . . .but they saw him
  . . .and cried out in fear!"   Mt 14:22-33; Mk 6:45-52

.*.*.*.   .*.*.*.   .*.*.*.

And after the resurrection
  he stood vaguely apparent
    in the pre-dawn mist
    at the water's edge
and shouted directions to them
  for a huge catch
    — and then he produced a fish of his own
      and some bread
        to serve a breakfast for them
        on the shore.   Jn 21:1-14

.*.*.*.   .*.*.*.   .*.*.*.

With more loyalty than information
  Peter firmly assured the temple tax collector
    that the Teacher
    paid the required tax;
and never gave the matter another thought
    until "Jesus spoke up first"
    and cleverly phrased a question
      to force Peter
      to recognize his error.

And so that his prized fisherman
  would never forget
    — Jesus sent him fishing
      for enough tax money for both of them.   Mt 17:24-26

. . .and for NOW   *. . .when we use humor*

— Humor has a way of relaxing students
  and aiding digestion of ideas
  as well as lunch.

— Like salt and scarlet, humor adds necessary flavor
  and color to learning, if used in proper amounts.

— An occasional turn of words, a look strategically timed
  can bring a chuckle, a shift of posture,
  and encourage alertness in our students.
  While they're waiting for the next light moment,
  some powerful lessons can be inserted.

— Humor should be light and free — never at the expense
  of a student's feelings.

Storytelling Techniques

Jesus was a born storyteller.
He seemed to tell stories most often
    when he was with small groups;
        sometimes among friends,
        but occasionally with his enemies.

Attention-holding plots
    were woven around some fascinating characters
      · in recognizable settings
            for his audience.

And he was a master
    at drawing the theme from his students:

            The Good Samaritan   Lk 10:25-37
            The Two Sons   Mt 21:28-32

The Evangelists recorded many instances
    where he simply told the story,
        concluded with the moral,
           and left the application
           in the hands of the listeners:

      The Pharisee and the Tax Collector   Lk 18:9-14
      The Workers in the Vineyard   Mt 20:1-16
      The Lost Sheep   Lk 15:4-7
      Parable of the Rich Fool   Lk 12:16-21

Occasionally
he even left the interpretation of the moral
    to his audience:
      The Lost Son   Lk 15:11-32
      The Rich Man and Lazarus   Lk 16:19-31
      Parable of the Gold Coins   Lk 19:12-27

But he made certain
    that Simon the Pharisee
    didn't miss the implication
        about the moneylender and his two debtors.
Not only Simon got the message;
    it must have been just as clear
    to Mary as she heard herself defended
        while she perfumed the Master's feet.   Lk 7:36-50

And it's a good thing
    the disciples weren't very sharp
        at grasping some of his stories.
Thanks to their openness
    in asking for further explanations
        he gave detailed interpretations
        of some thought-provoking parables:

      The Sower and the Seed   Lk 8:11-15
      The Widow and the Judge   Lk 18:1-8

The Shrewd Manager　　　　　　　　　　Lk 16:1-13
The Wheat and the Weeds　　　　　Mt 13:24-30, 36-43

Effective use
of both inductive and deductive teaching
　　　with stories!

Student-Involvement in Learning

One impressive lesson
　　　made such an impact on the apostles
　　　that all four evangelists
　　　　　contribute to the telling of it.
It must have lasted the better part of a day;
　　　and it's possible to find
　　　the integration of at least eight techniques
　　　　　that would pass the test
　　　　　of "master teaching".
　　　　　　　　　Mt 14:13-21; Mk 6:30-44; Lk 9:10-17; Jn 6:1-14

A long busy day of preaching
　　　was coming to an end.
The Teacher and his disciples
　　　hadn't had a moment to themselves,
　　　　　not even to eat.

Jesus had just suggested
　　　that they stop and rest for a while.
He was concerned
　　　about the welfare of his apostles,
　　　his student teachers.

But the crowds had followed them
　　　and he was concerned about them, too.

The disciples,
>evidently accustomed to having their opinions respected,
>>quickly suggested
>>that the crowds be dispersed
>>>to give them a chance to buy food.
But Jesus never missed an opportunity
>to prepare his apostles
>for their eventual assignment
>>of continuing his mission.

Too bad John didn't describe
>the expression in the Teacher's eyes
>when he said to Philip:

"Where can we buy enough food to feed all these people?"

It must have revealed
>at least some degree of teasing since:
>>"He said this to test Philip;
>>>*actually he already knew*
>>>what he would do."

It was a little early for testing,
>insufficient time
>to have mastered
>>the essentials of the lessons;
but maybe Philip had given evidence
>of being quicker than the others.
Obviously not —
>— Philip was still
>>on a beginner's level in Discipleship,
>>>although better at math.
He could see at a glance
>$200 worth of bread wouldn't be enough.

Andrew
    — who seemed to be an approachable man —
    was in the habit of bringing people to Jesus:
        first, his brother;
        then, Philip and some Greeks.
And this time he'd spotted a youngster
    with five loaves
    and a couple of fish.
Here, too, obviously not enough.

Satisfied that his apostles
    were at least trying their best
    to solve the problem
        using their own ingenuity and ability,
he gave them assistance. . .

     . . .*in organizing*
        — "Make the people sit down in rows, in groups of
           one hundred and of fifty."
        ("There was a lot of grass there" for the first
        parish picnic.)

     . . .*in doing ONLY what they could not do*
        — He took the bread and fish THAT THEY HAD PRODUCED.
        — He blessed them and broke them.

     . . .*in returning the ownership of the feast*
     back to his students
        — THEY distributed the food
        — THEY collected the leftovers.

And the apostles were awed
    by what they were able to do
        WITH HIM.

. . .and for NOW   *. . .when we involve our students*

— Are we more concerned about our students' needs
   or about our own?

—Do we give our students sufficient time and opportunity
   to try to solve problems before we offer some assistance
      — and then keep the assistance to a minimum?

— Are we satisfied to take a seat on the side while our students
   demonstrate their knowledge?

— Do we instill pride in our students by *using* what they
   contribute to their own learning?

— Do we keep our organization simple enough to permit our
   students to take command of their own learning?

Students-in-Trouble, concern for

He'd created a bit of havoc
      in the life of the man-born-blind
            by curing him.
The man had to begin his sight-life
      by facing people
            who doubted his identity
            and requested a continuous
            and tiring retelling
                  of how it had all happened
                        — neighbors, strangers, Pharisees.
Even his parents were put on the spot:
      "He is old enough; ask him."

The fellow must have thought the episode
      a closed issue

after his firm support
for the man
who "came from God"
and his subsequent expulsion from the Temple.

But it was then
that the Teacher came back.

The action of the Healing Teacher
had started all the man's problems,
so the Concerned Teacher
returned to calm the scene
and reward him
as only He could do.   Jn 9:1-41

. * . * . *.   . * . * . *.   . * . * . *.

Jesus never hesitated
to defend his Twelve
when they were criticized unjustly.

— On a Sabbath day
the hungry disciples munched on wheat heads
that they picked
as they walked through the field.
When the indignant Pharisees
were scandalized at such Sabbath-abuse
he defended the Twelve
with a reference to the great King David
and set the accusers straight
about the Sabbath.   Mt 12:1-8

— When eyebrows were raised
about his disciples' eating and drinking
while disciples of others fasted,
he explained their actions
with his bridegroom parable.   Lk 5:33-35

— The Pharisees also questioned
   the disciples' eating
      without properly washing their hands.
   And he counter-questioned them:
      "And why do you disobey God's command
        and follow your own teaching?"   Mt 15:1-3

— Once they were even accused
   of being too noisy
      when they were preparing for a celebration.
        (and what K-12 teacher hasn't heard the same!)
   His response?

      "If they keep quiet, I tell you,
      the stones themselves will shout."   Lk 19:37-40

— He even worked a miracle
   to protect Peter
      from facing the consequence
      of an impulsive swing of the sword.
   (Great motive, wrong action!)   Jn 18:10-11; Lk 22:49-51

         . * . * . *.   . * . * . *.   . * . * . *.

Twice he defended Mary,
   the sister of Martha and Lazarus.
      — once when she preferred
        listening at his feet
          to housekeeping tasks for his visit,   Lk 10:38-41

      — and once when she was extravagant
        with a pint of perfume
        which she poured over his feet.   Jn 12:1-7

Both times he came to her rescue.
Her attention to him was rewarded.

. . .and for NOW   *. . .when our students are in trouble*

— Students need to know their teacher will come
   to their defense if they are unjustly accused.

   And if they are guilty,
   they need to know even more,
         their teacher will be just as present
         with support and advice.

   We must be present to our students
   according to their needs.

— He told His Twelve:
   "I do not call you servants. . .
         . . .Instead, I call you friends."   Jn 15:15

QUALITIES OF THE MASTER TEACHER

Part Five

QUALITIES OF THE MASTER TEACHER

Although the only personal qualities
    the Teacher specifically told the disciples
    they should learn from him
        were gentleness and humility   Mt 11:29
he gave ample evidence
    of possessing many more traits
    that are worthy of imitation
        by any teacher.

HE WAS GENTLE, RESPECTFUL, and FORGIVING with those
    who had surrendered to a misguided heart:
        the woman caught in adultery;
        the one who'd had five husbands;
        Mary, the prostitute

        — forgiving the action, but not condoning it
        — "Go, but do not sin again."   Jn 8:11

HE WAS CONCERNED about HIS PUPILS' FAMILIES
    — even mothers-in-law!   Lk 4:38-39

HE MADE HIS STUDENTS FEEL IMPORTANT
    — He called them salt and light   Mt 5:13-16
    — He accepted an invitation
        to a dinner with outcasts
            to honor a new student.   Mt 9:9-13

HE PROTECTED the REPUTATION OF HIS STUDENTS
— even in his contacts with Judas:
"Hurry and do what you must!"
And none of the others knew
what the Teacher meant.   Jn 13:27-30
— His good shepherd parable was told to uphold
the tax collectors and outcasts
who listened to him.   Lk 15:1-7

HE WAS PRAYERFUL
— He began his teaching mission
with a forty-day retreat.   Lk 4:1-13
— He spent many nights in prayer in lonely places.

HE WAS AN INSPIRATION TO HIS STUDENTS
— "Make our faith greater."   Lk 16:5
— "Lord, teach us to pray. . ."   Lk 11:1

HE WAS FEARLESS in warning his students
of evil influence.
— "Watch out for the teachers of the Law. . ."   Mk 12:38-40

HE WAS TENDER, and LOVING
with the apostles
and Mary Magdalene
immediately after his resurrection,
as he led them from the shock of grief
to accept the astounding miracle of his rising
and to the realization that he was leaving them
with a God-sized mission to accomplish.

HE KNEW MEN'S HEARTS
— "There was no need
for anyone to tell him about men,
because he knew
what was in their hearts."   Jn 2:25

HE WAS PERCEPTIVE
— aware of his student's needs before
    the student expressed it   Lk 10:10-13
— He answered questions his students
    were too embarrassed to ask.   Jn 16:17-19
— He didn't force an answer when he knew they
    were ashamed to tell the truth.   Mk 9:32-33

HE WAS PATIENT with slower students
    and their naive questions.
— Throughout his last explanation
    at the supper he shared with them
    as he referred to his "going"
    they kept asking "where?"   Jn 16

HE WAS CAUTIOUS not to teach TOO MUCH TOO SOON
— "I have much more to tell you, *but now*
    it would be too much for you to bear."   Jn 16:12

HE PREPARED THEM ADEQUATELY for THE FINAL EXAM
— telling them precisely
    what questions to expect
    and how to answer them!   Mt 25:31-46

HE WAS PERFECT AT PACING A LESSON
— not too hurriedly, no matter how many detours
    he had to make to meet his students' needs.

HE EXPLAINED CLEARLY, with SIMPLE EXAMPLES
— "I tell you the truth. . ."
    . . .A man is born physically of human parents,
      but he is born spiritually of the Spirit."
    . . .This is how the judgment works. . ."   Jn 3:1-21

HE STARTED HIS TEACHING AT HIS STUDENTS'
READINESS POINT, no matter how elementary
— "What are you looking for?"

— "Where do you live, Teacher?"
— "Come and see." Jn 1:35-39
and he moved them forward!

HE SEARCHED for THE BEST WAY TO EXPLAIN
— "What shall we say the Kingdom of God is like?
. . .What parable shall we use to explain it?" Mk 4:30

HE WAS THOROUGH
— When the almost-cured blind man described people
as "trees walking around",
Jesus finished the job
— and "he saw all things clearly." Mk 8:22-26

HE WAS PRACTICAL
He noticed details overlooked by others.

— When the stunned crowd stood gaping
at Lazarus still bound up in his burial sheets
at the entrance of his tomb
Jesus told them:
"Untie him and let him go." Jn 11:44
— When Jairus' young daughter was called
back from the dead
he "ordered them
to give her something to eat". Lk 8:55

HE WAS KNOWLEDGEABLE about HIS SUBJECT MATTER
— "When the crowds heard this they
were amazed at his teaching." Mt 22:33
— ". . .he taught with authority" Mt 7:29
— Even his enemies wondered:
"How does this man know so much when
he has never been to school?" Jn 7:15
— ". . .all the people kept listening to him,
not wanting to miss a single word." Lk 19:48

HE WASN'T INTIMIDATED
    — when he had to teach a hard lesson   Mt 23:1-36
    — or when he faced students who
        rejected his message   Jn 10:1-40

HE WAS JUST, and EXPECTED JUSTICE FROM OTHERS
    — "If I have said something wrong,
        tell everyone here what it was.
        But if I am right in what I have said
        why do you hit me?"   Jn 18:23

    — He answered Pilate clearly and pointedly
        as the procurator tried to get the facts
        early in the inquiry.
            But Jesus was reluctant to answer
            after Pilate's wishy-washy response
            to the facts.   Jn 18:28-38; 19:8-11

HE WAS AVAILABLE
    — to the crowds   Jn 3:1-2
    — to those who needed his healing power   Mk 1:32-34
    — when he was tired   Mk 6
    — He prayed all night and in the early morning hours
        to leave the day for his ministry.   Jn 3:1-21

    — He seemed to have no office-hour limitations!

HE WAS PRUDENTLY CAUTIOUS
    — disappearing in the midst of the crowd
        who wanted to throw him over the cliff,
        because he had much more work to do!   Lk 4:28-30
    — choosing not to "go openly" when he knew
        the timing wasn't right   Jn 11:54

HE WAS SHARP, ALERT, KEEN with those
    who set out to entrap him

— shrewdly wording questions
  to confound them · · · · · · · · · · · · · · · · · Lk 20:26; Mt 21:23-27
— seeing through their motives · · · · · · · · · · · · · · · · · Mt 22:18
— parrying question for question · · · · · · · · · · · · · · · Mt 12:10-11

HE WAS STERN and ANGRY
  —when he dealt with hardened evil,
    with those who had no respect
      for his Father's House · · · · · · · · · · · · · · · · · · · Jn 2:13-22
— when his disciples scolded those
    who brought their children to him · · · · · · · · · · · · Mk 10:13-15

. * . * . * .   . * . * . * .   . * . * . * .

An outstanding quality
  of the Master Teacher
    was his adamant stand
      on specific issues of morality.

He expected his students
  to live
  according to a clear-cut code of action
  based on strong beliefs.
So he explained those principles
in definite, precise language;
  he answered questions on them
  to clarify misunderstandings;
    and he applied them to daily life.

Most importantly,
  it was evident that he lived what he taught:

— about anger · · · · · · · · · · · · · · · · · · · Mt 5:21-26
— about judging others · · · · · · · · · · · · · · · · Mt 7:1-5
— about love of enemies · · · · · · · · · · · · · · Mt 5:43-48

— about performing religious acts
in public   Mt 6:1-4
— about prayer   Mt 6:5-15; 7:7-12; Lk 11:5-13
— about revenge   Mt 5:38-42

His position was just as unyielding
on the current issues of his time:

     — on the Law   Mt 5:17-20
     — on adultery   Mt 5:27-28
     — on divorce   Mt 5:31-32; 19:1-10; Mk 10:2-12
     — on fasting   Mt 6:16-18
     — on material wealth   Mt 6:19-21; Lk 12:22-34

. * . * . * .   . * . * . * .   . * . * . * .

The Teacher
was revolutionary in his teachings.

He demanded
far more than the minimum requirements
of the Law,
and he made no apologies for it.

"You have heard that it was said. . .
. . .*but now I tell you*. . ."   Mt 5-7

. . .*and for NOW*   . . .*when we examine our own "teacher qualities"*

— Our students deserve to see what is in store for them
if they follow our teaching.
We are that best example.

— The principles we give our students
    must flow from solid beliefs.
    Consequently those principles
        must be broad enough
            to become the foundation
                for the structure of daily living,
      and clear enough
            to give a dependable sense of direction
                in matters which develop
                    as our society changes.

— We need to teach them
        HOW TO think
        HOW TO raise questions
        HOW TO offer opinions
        HOW TO read and listen
        HOW TO speak and write
        HOW TO evaluate
        HOW TO come to valid conclusions
        HOW and WHEN TO lead
        HOW and WHEN TO follow

— And we need to provide
    many opportunities to practice
        all these lessons
        on all levels
            — pre-school through university.

The *facts* they practice on
        may appear to be simple or unimportant;
        they may even become obsolete,

            but the *HOW-TO skills* will grow stronger
                — ready to serve them
            in each new NOW.

PART SIX

A LOOK AT HIS TEACHER

Jesus

Part Six

A LOOK AT HIS TEACHER

It's been said
  that teachers tend to teach
  the way they were taught
  when they were children,
    rather than the way
    they were taught to teach.

If that's true,
  it should be enlightening
  to look at the person
    who influenced the Teacher the most
      — HIS MOTHER.

    . * . * . . * . * . . * . * .

When the Nazarenes
  were trying to determine
    the source of his wisdom
they asked:

    "Isn't he the carpenter's son?
    Isn't Mary his mother?
     . . .Where did he get all this?"   Mt 13:54-57

And they rejected him.

Mary

Evidently,
    the carpenter and his wife
        hadn't been outstanding,
        nothing noteworthy about *their* education;
            so, whence his?

But the evangelists
    give us some clues
    about what he must have learned
        from her. . .

    . . .She must have shared with her all-knowing Son
        the story of her whole-hearted willingness
        to be the "Lord's servant".   Lk 1:38

    . . .He surely knew about his mother's
        three month visit to assist
        her elderly cousin before his own birth.   Lk 1:39-56

    . . .He'd been aware of her respect for
        and compliance with the Law each year
        as the family made the annual
        Passover Feast journey to Jerusalem.   Lk 1:41

    . . .He easily would recall his mother's
        straightforward reaction to his prolonged
        Temple visit when he was twelve:
            "Son, why have you done this to us?
            Your father and I have been terribly
            worried trying to find you."   Lk 1:48

        . * . * .   . * . * .   . * . * .

During his first thirty years
    she'd grown to know him well enough
    to be certain

that if she'd make him aware of a problem,
    he'd do something about it.
So, at Cana's wedding event of the season
    she found it necessary
    to speak only ten words —
        — five to him:
            "They are out of wine"
        — five to the servants:
            "Do whatever he tells you."

She knew him —

    — knew he'd be as concerned as she about
        the embarrassing situation for the newlyweds

    — knew that his don't-rush-me comment
        wasn't a final word

    — knew that he would take some action

    — knew that she wanted to do what she could to help
        . . .so she did some front-running for him

And nothing more
    is mentioned about her
    on this occasion,
        except that after the reception
    she accompanied her son,
        his disciples and some relatives
            for a few days' stay at Capernaum.   Jn 2:1-12

. * . * .   . * . * .   . * . * .

She visited him
    at least once when he was teaching,
    but no details are given
        about their meeting.   Mt 12:46-48

. * . * . * .   . * . * . * .   . * . * . * .

She is mentioned
 as "standing close to Jesus' cross"
  — when the sight of her
   would afford him some support.
And in his dying moments
 he was conscious
 of providing for his mother,
    his friend,
    his teacher.

   "And from that time the disciple
    took her to live in his home."   Jn 19:25-27

. * . * . * .   . * . * . * .   . * . * . * .

Luke mentions her by name
 one final time in his Acts,
  recording how she
   was among the little band
   of his followers
 who went "to pray as a group".   Ac 1:14

. * . * . * .   . * . * . * .   . * . * . * .

From all that's recorded of her,
 his teacher seems to have been. . .

   . . .simple and unassuming
   . . .devoutly religious
   . . .very economical with words
   . . .able to instill confidence
   . . .a loving woman, concerned about others' needs
   . . .trusting of her student

. . .interested in his mission without being interfering
. . .accepting of his friends and his mission
. . .willing to watch him from the sidelines

A person who chooses
        any teacher-education program
        always takes a chance
                — never being really certain
                        of the quality of instruction,
                                the practicality of the learning.
Not so,
        in the case of the Master Teacher.

He designed his own "program"
        and apparently never had any reason
                to regret it
                or to redesign it!

TEACHER

TEACHER

He could have chosen any planet
    in any of the countless solar systems
        he had designed

        . . .but he chose ours
           and he spent thirty-three years with us.

He could have chosen any period
    in our earth-history
        as the most effective one
        for getting his Good News spread

        . . .but he chose a time
           BEFORE so many great inventions
              were even imagined
          — before satellite communication
          — before television
              — even before radio
          — before word processors
          — before typewriters
              — even before electricity
              — even before printing

      . . .but he chose a time
         when his original team of messengers
           could travel only on foot
           or by ox-cart
           or by sea-vessels powered only
              by men's muscles.

He could have chosen any place
  as his headquarters:
    Rome, Corinth, Antioch, Alexandria
      — all great cities when he came,
    or a continent not yet discovered in the years B.C.

        . . .but he chose to spend thirty years
          of preparation
          in a no-place: Nazareth,
          and "Can anything good come from Nazareth?"

He could have spent his final three years
  — as a statesman,
      influencing governments and world powers
  — as a physician,
      curing all the diseases of his time
  — as a synagogue leader,
      establishing his teachings
        among educated churchmen
  — as a renowned social reformer,
      founding a whole new social system

        . . .but he chose to be a Teacher
          — to mold characters
          — to shape human destinies
          — to influence families
          — to affect future generations
          — to influence neighborhoods,
                          cities,
                              nations,
                                  the world
          — to spread the Kingdom of his Father.

He closed his thirty-three years
  by directing that his followers:
    "Go to the whole world
      and preach the Gospel
        to all mankind."   Mk 16:15

And "The disciples went and preached everywhere,
    and the Lord worked with them
    and proved that their preaching was true
        by giving them the sign of power."   Mk 16:20

His disciples' disciples,
    multiplied again and again and again,
        are motivated by his promise:
        "I will be with you always
            to the end of the age."   Mt 28:20

And they spend their days TEACHING
    — inspired by the life,
            the message,
            the methods,
                of JESUS, THE MASTER TEACHER.

INDEX

INDEX